SCHOLASTIC

AF650321

Mastering Science 2

Name ______________________________

Class ______________________________

Photo attributions and credits:

Speech Bubble: Amada44(http://commons.wikimedia.org/wiki/File:Speech_bubble.svg).
pp.6-7: All other images from Fables; except the following which are from Wikimedia commons: LeuschteLampe(http://commons.wikimedia.org/wiki/File:Farbverlauf_Augenfarben.jpg). p.8: All other images from Fables. pp.19-21: All other images from Fables. p.26: All other images from Fables. p.29: All other images from Fables; except the following which are from Wikimedia commons: Tallguy1982(http://commons.wikimedia.org/wiki/File:Man_Sweating_MIN.jpg). pp.30-31: All other images from Fables. pp.32-33: All other images from Fables; except the following which are from Wikimedia commons: T. R. Shankar Raman(http://commons.wikimedia.org/wiki/File:Village_banyan.JPG), MyName (MKFF (talk)(http://commons.wikimedia.org/wiki/File:Appletree_2.jpg), Rameshng(http://commons.wikimedia.org/wiki/File:Thotapuri_Mango_tree_in_Kolar.JPG)
pp.34-35: All other images from Fables; except the following which are from Wikimedia commons:4028mdk09(http://commons.wikimedia.org/wiki/File:Gef%C3%BCllte_rote_Rose_Nu%C3%9Floch.JPG), User: Marco.Finke(http://commons.wikimedia.org/wiki/File:Gras2.jpg), Enoch Lau(http://commons.wikimedia.org/wiki/File:Pumpkin_with_stalk.jpg), Biswarup Ganguly(http://commons.wikimedia.org/wiki/File:Epipremnum_aureum_-_Kolkata_2011-09-24_5720.JPG), pp.40-41: The following images are from Wikimedia commons: Rasbak(http://commons.wikimedia.org/wiki/File:Phaseolus_vulgaris_white_beans,_witte_boon.jpg), Sanjay Achary(http://commons.wikimedia.org/wiki/File:Chana.jpg), Sanjay Acharya (http://commons.wikimedia.org/wiki/File:Kidney_beans.jpg), User: Henningklevjer (http://commons.wikimedia.org/wiki/File:JasmineRice.jpg), Thamizhpparithi Maari(http://commons.wikimedia.org/wiki/File:A_closeup_scene_of_wheat..JPG), Spedona(http://commons.wikimedia.org/wiki/File:Pommes_de_terre_Monalisa.png), Rufino Uribe(http://commons.wikimedia.org/wiki/File:Cut_sugarcane.jpg), Kander (http://commons.wikimedia.org/wiki/File:Carrots.JPG), User: Mbdortmund(http://commons.wikimedia.org/wiki/File:210704_rettich-raphanus-sativus-marktware_1-640x480.jpg), Peter Presslein(http://commons.wikimedia.org/wiki/File:Brassica_rapa_turnip.jpg), Epukas (http://commons.wikimedia.org/wiki/File:Cabbage_Estonia.jpg), Victor M. Vicente Selvas (http://commons.wikimedia.org/wiki/File:Espinac_5nov.JPG), Flickr: Grand Rapids Lettuce(http://commons.wikimedia.org/wiki/File:Grand_Rapids_Lettuce.jpg). pp.42-43: All other images from Fables; except the following which are from Wikimedia commons: http://www.flickr.com/photos/calliope (http://commons.wikimedia.org/wiki/File:Cauliflowerr.jpg), User: David.Monniaux (http://commons.wikimedia.org/wiki/File:Broccoli_DSC00861.png), Luc Viatour
(http://commons.wikimedia.org/wiki/File:Tomates_cerises_Luc_Viatour.jpg), Ashlyak(http://commons.wikimedia.org/wiki/File:Grape.JPG), Mschel (http://commons.wikimedia.org/wiki/File:Banana.png), © 2005 by Tomasz Sienicki(http://commons.wikimedia.org/wiki/File:Kt_xx_0011_ubt.jpeg), Colin Smith(http://commons.wikimedia.org/wiki/File:A_Fine_Pair_-_geograph.org.uk_-_916522.jpg), NobbiP(http://commons.wikimedia.org/wiki/File:Pear_r%C3%B6tliche_85.jpg). pp.44-45: All other images from Fables; except the following which are from Wikimedia commons: User:健ちゃん(http://commons.wikimedia.org/wiki/File:Paper_Packaging_paper.JPG), annieo76 (http://commons.wikimedia.org/wiki/File:Bamboo_Forest.jpg), WikiCantona (http://commons.wikimedia.org/wiki/File:Flip_flop.jpg), Laurensazx (http://commons.wikimedia.org/wiki/File:Jutebag.jpg), Tamorlan (http://commons.wikimedia.org/wiki/File:Yute_-_Sacos.jpg), Scott Ehardt(http://commons.wikimedia.org/wiki/File:Toothpaste.jpg), מודנר (http://commons.wikimedia.org/wiki/File:Head_%26_Shoulders_shampoo_bottle.jpg), Thesupermat(http://commons.wikimedia.org/wiki/File:Billes_de_bois_sur_le_bord_d%27une_route_-_003.JPG), Fyndtorget(http://commons.wikimedia.org/wiki/File:Bord.jpg), 4028mdk09(http://commons.wikimedia.org/wiki/File:Buntes_Holzspielzeug_2011.JPG), Noah Elhardt(http://commons.wikimedia.org/wiki/File:Sarracenia_rubra_ne.JPG), Stefano Zucchinali(http://commons.wikimedia.org/wiki/File:Digested_fly.JPG). p.49: All other images from Fables; except the following which are from Wikimedia commons: DemonTraitor(http://commons.wikimedia.org/wiki/File:Grey_squirrel.jpg), Markus Braun(http://commons.wikimedia.org/wiki/File:Zwergzebu-01.jpg). p.50: All other images from Fables; except the following which are from Wikimedia commons: Tony Hisgett (http://commons.wikimedia.org/wiki/File:Snow_Monkeys.jpg), monkeywing
(http://commons.wikimedia.org/wiki/File:Golden_sebright_cockerel.jpg), User:Robek(http://commons.wikimedia.org/wiki/File:Pair_of_lions_v2.jpg), rbennett661(http://commons.wikimedia.org/wiki/File:Pet_dog_in_Wales,_United_Kingdom-3April2010.jpg), User: Artic(http://commons.wikimedia.org/wiki/File:Bee_With_Pollen.jpg), Shahnoor Habib Munmun(http://commons.wikimedia.org/wiki/File:Bee_Hives_Bangladesh.JPG), Ernst Vikne(http://commons.wikimedia.org/wiki/File:Norwegian_hen.jpg), Lilly M(http://commons.wikimedia.org/wiki/File:Bombyx_mori_001.JPG), B-nji3 (http://commons.wikimedia.org/wiki/File:Ratemisa.JPG). p.56: Image from Wikimedia commons: NikoLang(http://commons.wikimedia.org/wiki/File:Celestia_sun.jpg), p.58: The following image is from Wikimedia commons: User:(http://commons.wikimedia.org/wiki/File:Full_moon.png). p.70: The following image is from Wikimedia commons: Haham hanuka(http://commons.wikimedia.org/wiki/File:Earth_Eastern_Hemisphere.jpg). p.71: The following images are from Wikimedia commons: Tyw7(http://commons.wikimedia.org/wiki/File:Plaintrain.JPG), Vinod Panicker(http://commons.wikimedia.org/wiki/File:Camel_cart_in_Rann_of_Kutch.jpg), Dead habbits(http://commons.wikimedia.org/wiki/File:Spiti_In_Himachal_Pradesh.jpg). p.72: The following images are from Wikimedia commons: Hiranmay(http://commons.wikimedia.org/wiki/File:SuryaTaal.jpg), Nigel Brown(http://commons.wikimedia.org/wiki/File:Final_slopes_of_Beinn_Fhada_-_geograph.org.uk_-_500864.jpg)

This edition specially created for Scholastic India.

First edition 2012
Reprinted 2012, 2014 (thrice), 2015, 2016, 2017, 2019, 2020, 2022, 2023, 2025

ISBN 978-81-8477-926-4
Printed in India at Sai Printo Pack Pvt. Ltd.

Contents

 ISBN 978-81-8477-926-4

Introduction

Mastering Science is an exciting science series for levels 1 to 8. The books have been designed to fulfill the requirements of the National Curriculum Framework (NCF), which has been adopted by CBSE, ICSE and major State Educational Boards.

The series adopts a learner-centred approach, encouraging students to make connections between their role in their immediate environment and the world around them. The coursebooks are filled with lots of colourful photographs and illustrations that expose students to real-life everyday experiences from around the world.

In addition, the series prepares students to meet the challenges of the future by

- following pyramidal pedagogy
- encouraging exploration and innovation
- facilitating observation and logical analysis to support conclusions
- promoting independent learning

Learn More provides activities that hone the students' ability to absorb, infer, classify, experiment and predict.

Explore encourages students to analyse and question.

Learn More

Go for a nature walk around the garden or park. List all the things you hear, see, feel and smell.

I hear	I see	I feel	I smell

Explore

Observe the way in which popcorn is made. Yes No

Can you hear the kernels pop?

Can you smell the popcorn?

Can you see the popcorn?

Did you taste the popcorn?

KEEPING HEALTHY

To be strong and fit, we must eat healthy food, drink clean water and keep our homes, school and surroundings clean.

14

I Care provides value education in levels 1 to 3.

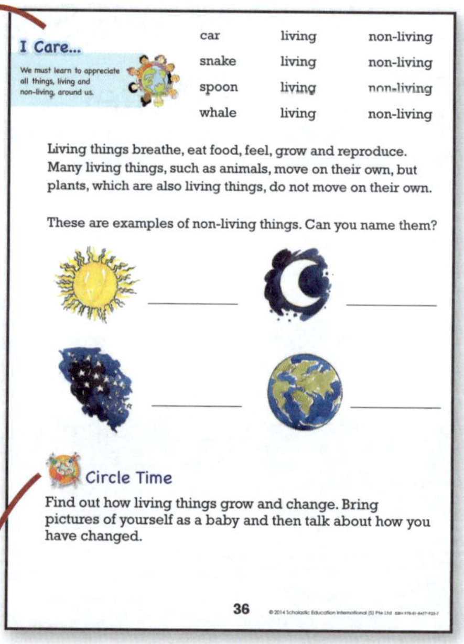

I Care...

We must learn to appreciate all things, living and non-living, around us.

car	living	non-living
snake	living	non-living
spoon	living	non-living
whale	living	non-living

Living things breathe, eat food, feel, grow and reproduce. Many living things, such as animals, move on their own, but plants, which are also living things, do not move on their own.

These are examples of non-living things. Can you name them?

Circle Time

Find out how living things grow and change. Bring pictures of yourself as a baby and then talk about how you have changed.

36

Circle Time promotes exchange of ideas and techniques while laying emphasis on working as a team.

 ISBN 978-81-8477-926-4

Quiz Time

1. Answer the questions.
   a. What is a galaxy? Name a few.
   b. List the components of the solar system.
   c. List a few uses of man-made satellites.
   d. What are terrestrial planets? Name them.
   e. Which planets are known as the gas giants and why?
   f. Is the Sun bigger than the Moon?
   g. Does the Moon give out light?
   h. Describe how the Sun affects the seasons on Earth.
   i. As night falls in India, is it night all over the world? Explain.
   j. Why does the Sun seem to disappear at night?
   k. Why does the Sun appear to move across the sky?
2. Fill in the blanks with the correct words from the brackets.
   a. The Moon orbits the __________. (Earth/Sun/stars)
   b. Groups of stars are called __________. (Milky Way/constellations/galaxy)
   c. The Earth orbits the __________. (Moon/Sun/Venus)
   d. The __________ is a natural satellite of the Earth. (Sun/Mercury/Moon)
   e. It takes twenty-four hours to complete one __________. (rotation/revolution/orbit)

104

3. Fill in the blanks to complete the sentences.

The Earth spins on its axis every __________ hours. Because of this spin, the Sun appears to rise in the __________ and set in the __________. While the Earth is spinning, the side that faces the Sun has __________.

4. Match the words with the correct definitions.

a.	axis	the force that pulls matter towards the centre of the Earth
b.	gravity	when it appears that the Sun is going down in the west
c.	sunset	an imaginary line running through the poles of the Earth
d.	orbit	when it appears that the Sun has risen in the east
e.	sunrise	the path an object takes around another object in space
f.	solar system	a shape like a ball
g.	sphere	the system of planets, along with the Sun, around which they revolve

Do you know the shape of the Earth? Support your answer with examples.

105

Quiz Time tests knowledge retention and serves as a quick recap of the lesson.

Higher Order Thinking Skills (HOTS) questions are included in levels 4 and above. These questions sharpen the students' skills of making inferences, understanding the logic behind a concept and thinking outside the box.

Learn More

Find out more information about why earthworms are known as friends of farmers.

Factastic
Weeds have a fibrous root system. This makes it very hard to pull them out of the ground. Pulled out weeds may grow back from any roots that may have been left behind in the soil.

Stem

The stem is the main part of the shoot, which bears the leaves, buds and flowers. The stem transports water and nutrients from the roots to all parts of the plant and supports the weight of the plant. It also carries food made by the leaves to all parts of the plant.

Leaves

Leaves grow on stems. They are responsible for converting sunlight into food through photosynthesis and respiration. Leaves store food and water for the plant.

respiration: the act of inhalation and exhalation of air; breathing

Factastic
The leaf is known as the kitchen of the plant as it makes food for the plant.

14

New and difficult words are defined in the **glossary.**

Factastic imparts interesting information and facts related to the topic under discussion.

How to Make a Project

Science experiments and projects (and presentations) are a fantastic ... engage in hands-on learning experiences. They enhance reasoning ... the curiosity of the students.

1. Title – For a science project, choose a catchy title. The title co... project. It is crucial to state the essential purpose of the project...
2. Introduction and Purpose – This section introduces the topic ... information already available and states the purpose of the proj... this topic and include citations (if any) in this section.
3. The Hypothesis or Question – Use this section to state your ... that the project aims to address.
4. Materials and Methods – All the materials used in the project ... may also describe the entire procedure used to perform the pro...
5. Data and Results – Data refers to the actual numbers or othe... project. This information can be presented in tables or charts. ... data is used to reach the conclusion.
6. Conclusion – The focus of the conclusion should be to answer th... Here, the data and its results should be compared and its findings ...

Alternatively, you may use the format below while starting out with ...

project planning
Choose a subject.
Research information on the Internet or at the library.
Study the information/data collected.
Make a plan for the topic selected.
Collect material required. (Most of the material required can be procured from around the house. Others may be easily available in retail stores.)
Set up and perform experiments.
Record data.
Analyse data.
Write a summary.
In case of a presentation: • shop for a poster board and display materials • print out final copies of your work • put together the board presentation
TOTAL (Add up the total estimated hours.)

137

How to Use an Encyclopedia

An encyclopedia is a useful resource found in all libraries. An encyclopedia may be a single volume, subject specific, or multi volume cover... Because encyclopedias are so easy to use and so ac... encyclopedias as their first option for a reference tool.

Most general encyclopedias are multivolume sets and ar... format. Some encyclopedias may need you to know the ... in order to find specific information covered over a variety... encyclopedias devote separate volumes to different subj...

Locate the index. The index is usually in the last series o... alphabetical order. It gives you page numbers and volum... article you are researching.

Read the article and pick out relevant information for you...

For teachers

A. Pass a volume of an encyclopedia to a group of students. Ask them to go through the layout, the way the information is organised and the quickest way to locate an entry. Challenge each group to compile an encyclopedia on any topic. Topics could be children's authors, unique inventions, historical sites in Asia, etc.

B. Ask the students to read an entry on any animal of their choice. Encourage the students to write a newspaper article or a poem using all the details and facts from the entry.

Pink is my nose
I thrive on garbage
Go away, my friend

Tips
- Look out fo... can broade... insight into...
- Pay attenti... pictures in t...
- The outline... is a helpful ... organising ...
- Refer to au... information ... introductory...

138

How to Use the Internet

One of the most recent and popular resource for research is the Internet. The Internet is a repository of information collected from various sources. Navigating through sites and links can give you updated information. Though the Internet is a wealth of information, before proceeding on any topic, take an adult's help to determine which sites might be reliable and which might not be a good source.

For teachers

Divide the class into four groups. Give three groups a topic to research and present. These groups will have different resources to research. The fourth group will then review the depth and breadth of the information, and survey and compare all the sources. They can present their report based on:

Which source gave you more information?

Which source gave you better information?

Tips
- It is a good idea to sit with an adult and bookmark the sites that you will need for research. This way you can directly go to the pages you want to view.
- Before beginning the topic, write down some keywords on which you will base your research.
- Use quality, child-friendly search engines such as www.ajkids.com (Ask Jeeves Kids) and www.yahooligans.com (Yahooligans!). You can keep a list of helpful sites near the computer for easy access.
- Quotation marks are important while conducting a topic search. If you enter your topic or key words without quotation marks around it, the search will give information about anything linked to the words. If you put the search topic in quotation marks, you will get information related to the exact words placed within quotation marks.
- If you can't read through the entire article, you can use the FIND option to locate a particular word in the article.

139

Students are taught to use an atlas, the encyclopedia and the Internet in levels 3 to 5 to do basic research, individually and in groups, to present reports and projects. These help build the ability to learn independently.

 ISBN 978-81-8477-926-4

1
MY BODY

Though most human beings have similar bodies, it is important to remember that no two people look the same. Each one is different from the other. Each one of us is unique.

Everyone has different facial features. Some people have thick lips while others may have thin or small lips. Look at the different shapes and colours of eyes.

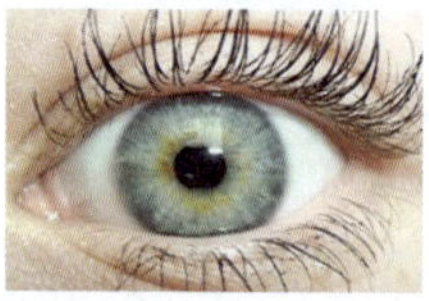
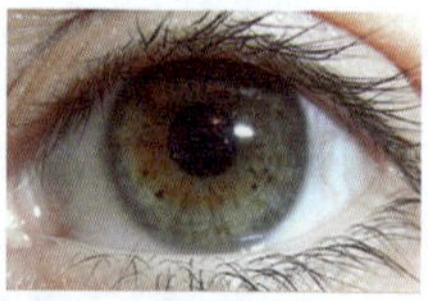
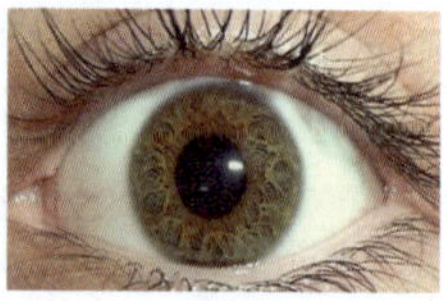

Use the describing words below to write about your friend's features. Tick (✓) the correct option as you observe your friend.

taller than me	yes	no
eye colour	brown	black
ears	big	small
nose	pointed	round
hair colour	brown	black
fingers	long	small

 ISBN 978-81-8477-926-4

Circle Time

Look in the mirror and observe your arms, hands, legs, feet, face, hair, ears and nose. How are you different from your friends? Discuss with the class.

Explore

How long is Bala's foot? _______cm

How long is your foot? ______ cm

Is your foot shorter than Bala's? ____

Find out the foot sizes of three of your friends.

name	foot size
me	
friend 1	
friend 2	
friend 3	

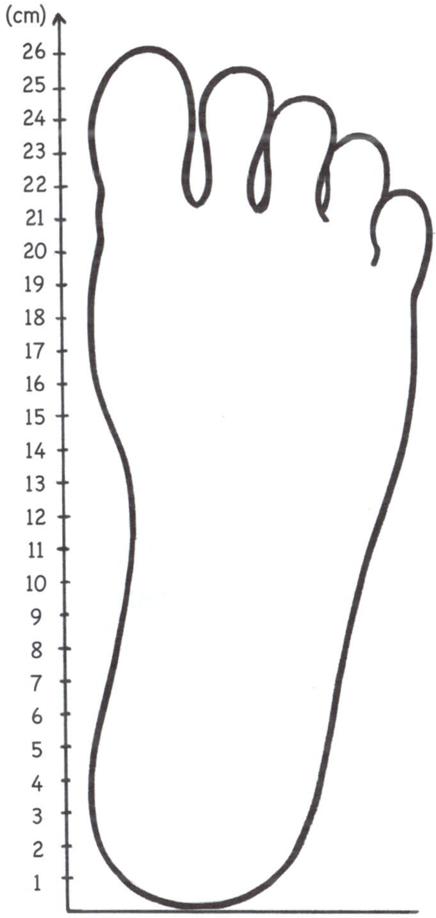

Bala's foot

Factastic

Twins are two people who are born at the same time to the same mother. Often they look the same and it is not easy to tell them apart. But there are some twins who do not look like one another. They are called fraternal twins.

 ISBN 978-81-8477-926-4

Learn More

People from different countries look different from one another. There are about 5,000 million people in the world. Each year about 90 million more are born. Look at the picture below. These children are all different, but they are similar in some ways.

They are similar because ______________________________

____

____

____

They are different because ____________________________

____

____

____

 ISBN 978-81-8477-926-4

THE SKELETON

Our body has a frame made up of 206 bones. This frame is known as the **skeleton**.

The skeleton protects the internal organs of our body. It supports and holds the body up. The skeleton is covered with muscles and skin.

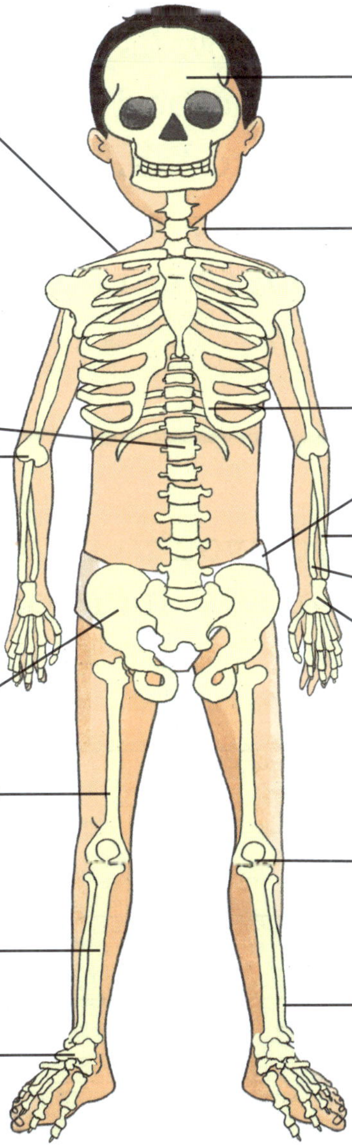

spinal cord: a bundle of nerves that sends information from the brain to the rest of the body

 ISBN 978-81-8477-926-4

Muscles are found under the skin and are attached to the bones. They help move our bones so that we can run, walk, dance and play. We need muscles to smile, wink and even to scratch our nose. There are 600 muscles in our body.

Put your hands on your face and smile. Observe and feel the muscles working.

The body parts that bend are known as **joints**. The joint is the place where two bones come together. Some joints move and others don't. Moving joints allow us to eat, play, twist, bend, and move different parts of the body. The elbows and knees are joints which help bend and then straighten the arms and legs. Fingers and toes also have joints which allow movement. Some other examples of joints are neck, shoulder and hip.

Learn More

When you pick up a pencil you're using the bones in your fingers, hand, wrist and arm. Which joints are used when you do these actions?

looking sideways ____________________

waving goodbye ____________________

kicking a ball ____________________

drawing a sketch ____________________

touching your toes ____________________

nodding your head ____________________

 ISBN 978-81-8477-926-4

raising your arm ______________________

sitting cross-legged ______________________

Posture is the way we sit, stand or walk.

Always keep your back straight while sitting, standing or playing. Walk and sit with your back upright, shoulders straight and head high.

Tick (✓) the picture that depicts good posture.

☐

☐

☐

I Care...

We need to exercise our muscles to stay healthy and to grow strong.

 ISBN 978-81-8477-926-4

Internal Organs

The parts inside our bodies are known as **internal organs**.

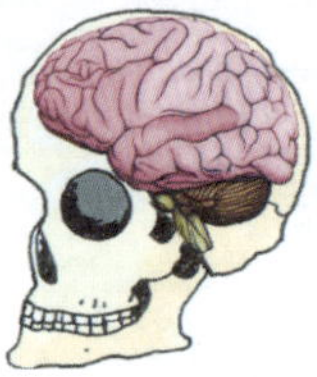

The **brain** tells the body what to do. The brain is inside the bony frame of our head, known as the skull. The brain helps us to think, breathe, move, speak, see, hear, play music and draw. It also helps us to show emotions. It is the control centre of the body.

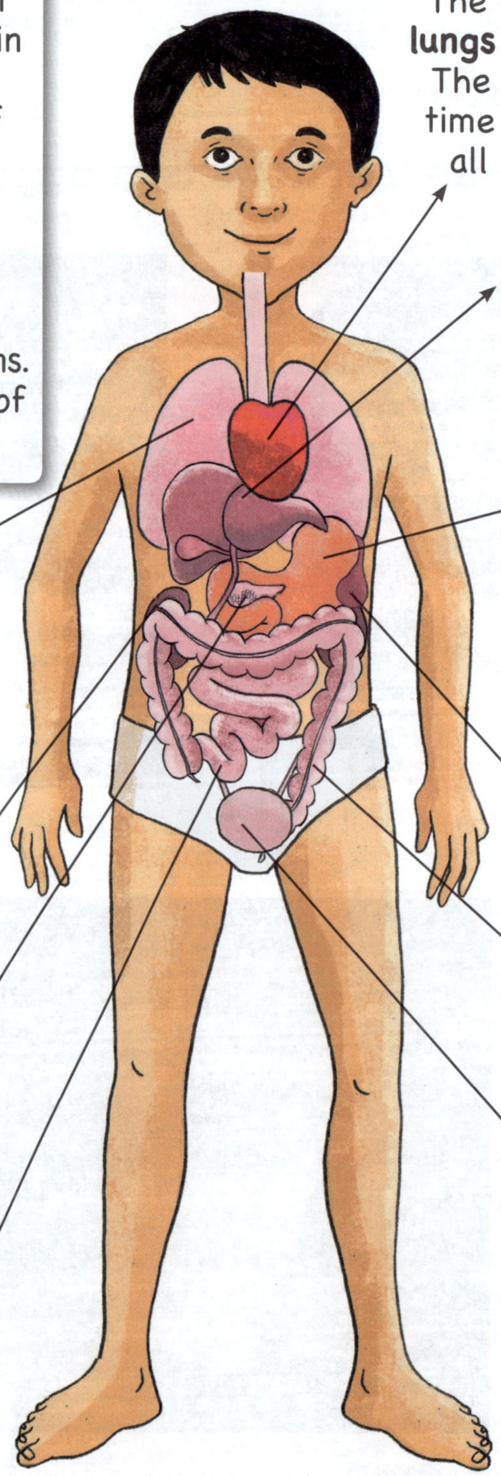

The **heart** and a pair of **lungs** are inside our chest. The heart beats all the time and pumps blood to all parts of the body.

The **liver** processes food and cleans the blood.

The **lungs** are close to the heart. Lungs help the body to breathe. Air goes into the body through the nostrils. It goes into the lungs and the used air comes out of the nostrils.

Below the chest is the **stomach**, which contains acid that breaks down the food.

The **spleen** helps make blood cells.

The **kidneys** clean waste from the blood and turn it into urine.

The **large intestine** turns food waste into poop.

The **pancreas** helps control the sugar in the blood.

The **bladder** stores urine.

The **small intestine** absorbs vitamins, minerals and other nutrients from food.

 ISBN 978-81-8477-926-4

Explore

Find out how long you can hold your breath. Use a digital clock to record this. How did you feel after this activity?

Held breath for ____________ seconds.

Sense Organs

The eyes, ears, nose, tongue and skin are the five sense organs. They help us to see, hear, smell, taste and touch.

Sense of sight: We use our eyes to see what is happening around us.
Sense of hearing: Our ears pick up different sounds as we sit quietly and listen.
Sense of taste and smell: The nose and tongue work together so we can enjoy the food that we eat.
Sense of touch: The skin is the biggest organ in the human body. It tells us what it feels as we touch something.

Do you:	Yes	No
touch your eyes with dirty hands?	☐	☐
wash your hands often?	☐	☐
rub your eyes?	☐	☐
cut your nails regularly?	☐	☐
strain your eyes by watching too much TV?	☐	☐
eat healthy food?	☐	☐
keep your nose clean?	☐	☐

 ISBN 978-81-8477-926-4

Circle Time

Put on a blindfold. Ask your friend or teacher to place different objects on a table in front of you. Try feeling each object with your elbow. Can you tell which one is which? Now, feel the objects with your fingers. Are fingers or elbows better at feeling things? Give yourself two points for getting one object correct.

Quiz Time

1. Answer the questions.

a. Name three joints in the human body.

b. What is posture?

c. What is the skeleton?

d. What is the function of the skeleton?

e. What is a joint? Name any one joint.

f. What are internal organs? Name two internal organs.

2. Fill in the blanks with the correct words from the brackets.

a. The ______________________ is inside our chest. (stomach/heart/brain)

b. Food gets digested in the ______________________. (stomach/heart/brain)

c. ______________________ is the way we sit, stand or walk. (Posture/Muscles/Joint)

 ISBN 978-81-8477-926-4

d. We have ____________________ sense organs. (six/five/seven)

e. ____________________ help us to breathe. (Heart/Stomach/Lungs)

f. Body parts that bend are called ____________________. (muscles/joints/internal organs)

3. Fill in the blanks with the help of words given below.

bones	lungs	heart	straight	skeleton

a. The human body has a framework of ____________ known as the skeleton.

b. The ______________ is covered with muscles and skin.

c. The ______________ pumps blood throughout our body.

d. We should always keep a ______________ posture.

e. We have two ______________ that help us breathe.

4. Tick (✓) Yes if it is a good posture, No if it is not.

	Yes	No
a. straight back	☐	☐
b. drooping shoulders	☐	☐
c. head held high	☐	☐
d. straight shoulders	☐	☐
e. bent back	☐	☐
f. drooping head	☐	☐

 ISBN 978-81-8477-926-4

5. Unscramble the words in brackets and circle them in the word grid.

a. The food we eat goes here (maotshc)

b. This tells the body what to do (nriab)

c. We breathe through these (lirntsos)

d. Two bones meet here (ijnto)

e. The brain lies inside this (lkuls)

f. Parts inside our body (angros)

g. The air we breathe goes in these (gulns)

h. The heart and lungs are inside this (etsch)

n	s	t	o	m	a	c	h
o	j	t	r	n	h	t	s
s	o	j	g	b	h	y	k
t	i	l	a	r	n	h	u
r	n	u	n	a	f	u	l
i	t	n	s	i	d	g	l
l	o	g	q	n	d	f	d
s	n	s	c	h	e	s	t

 ISBN 978-81-8477-926-4

6. Find the answers.

a. This is a robot.  This is its control centre. 

What is yours? ____________________

b. This is a helmet.  It protects the head.

What protects your brain? ____________________

c. This is a blender.  It churns food.

What churns the food you eat? ____________________

d. This is a bike pump.  It pumps air into tyres.

What helps pump blood throughout your body?

____

 ISBN 978-81-8477-926-4

2
Food

We need food to grow and to remain healthy and strong. The food that we eat provides us with the energy to study, play and remain active.

We all have different food choices. Some people eat eggs, meat, fish and chicken. They are called **non-vegetarians**. People who do not eat meat, fish and chicken, but eat fruits and vegetables are called **vegetarians**. Those who do not eat any animal products, such as meat, milk, curd, cheese and butter, are called **vegans**.

We must eat different kinds of food. Each kind of food plays an important role in the development of the body. Eating different kinds of food in the right quantities will help us to stay healthy and strong.

 ISBN 978-81-8477-926-4

Food Groups

The important food groups are

1. **Starch and carbohydrates** give us energy and help the body grow. Wheat, rice, potatoes and bread are examples of such body-building foods which provide us the energy to do work. They break down very slowly releasing energy.

2. **Vitamins and minerals** found in fruits, vegetables and nuts protect us from diseases and fight germs. These are protective foods that keep the body working efficiently.
3. **Proteins** are body builders and repairers. Proteins are particularly important for growth. Fish, milk, eggs, meats and nuts help build muscle strength.
4. **Calcium** helps us develop strong teeth and bones.
5. **Fat** keeps us warm and **sugar** gives us instant energy and helps us remain active. Cheese, butter, ghee and oil are examples of fats. Fat also protects our organs, such as kidneys, and helps absorb vitamins.

 ISBN 978-81-8477-926-4

The body goes through various changes. A healthy diet with a balance and variety of foods will help us cope with all these changes.

Balanced Meal

Factastic

Milk is white because it contains a white protein known as casein. Milk also contains fat, which is white.

It is very important that we eat a **balanced diet** so that we remain healthy. A balanced diet helps us grow, provides us energy and keeps us healthy and strong. Eating a balanced diet means consuming a wide variety of foods and drinks from all the food groups.

Factastic

In parts of China, many people eat insects. Some insects that are commonly eaten are bean worms, scorpions and locusts.

Circle Time

Discuss your favourite food from the food groups.

Unhealthy Food

Junk or **unhealthy food** is low in nutritional value. It is often high in fat, sugar and calories. A little bit is not bad but too much of unhealthy food may make us sick.

I Care...

We must not waste food. There are many people in the world who do not have enough food to eat.

 ISBN 978-81-8477-926-4

Learn More

Eating from only one food group or eating too much junk food may make you unwell, increase your weight or rot your teeth. Find out the other problems one may face by making unhealthy food choices.

Staying Healthy

You need to look after your body to keep it working properly. We need to exercise to stay healthy. Exercise is good for the heart and muscles and it keeps the joints flexible.

Yoga and other forms of exercise help us stay healthy.

Sound sleep of eight hours gives the body a chance to rest and repair itself.

Water has several important functions in the body. It helps maintain the body's temperature. Water helps flush out waste products and toxins. It helps nutrients travel to all parts of the body. It protects the joints. Water is good for the skin and helps the body process food more efficiently. Remember to drink plenty of water through the day.

> toxins: poisonous substances

It is important to keep germs away. Germs can make you ill. Remember to wash your hands before eating and after going to the toilet.

 ISBN 978-81-8477-926-4

Learn More

Classify the food items below as healthy or junk food. Write H for healthy or J for junk in the boxes.

 ISBN 978-81-8477-926-4

Paste pictures of foods that give energy and help you grow, and foods that help build and repair the body.

proteins: milk, fish, eggs, meat, beans, cheese, peas, nuts	fats, starch and carbohydrates: oil, butter, margarine, potato, bread, cereal, pasta, noodles, rice, sugar

 ISBN 978-81-8477-926-4

Learn More

Tick (✓) the good food habits.

- Eat street food often. ☐
- Eat fresh fruits and vegetables. ☐
- Wash fruits and vegetables well before eating them. ☐
- Eat at different times every day. ☐
- Eat alone in front of the television. ☐
- Eat only one food group every week. ☐
- Store cooked food outside the refrigerator. ☐
- Chew food properly. ☐
- Waste food. ☐
- Talk while eating. ☐
- Wash hands before eating. ☐
- Sit at the dining table to eat meals. ☐
- Never wash fruits and vegetables with water. ☐
- Cook food in clean vessels. ☐
- Overcook or burn food. ☐
- Keep food covered. ☐

 ISBN 978-81-8477-926-4

Foodborne Illnesses

Sometimes the food we eat makes us ill, a condition known as food poisoning. Food poisoning occurs when we eat food containing germs and bacteria. Food from animals, raw and unwashed fruits and vegetables may contain germs. To avoid food poisoning, we need to prepare, cook and store food properly.

Explore

Match the food to the plate.

 ISBN 978-81-8477-926-4

Quiz Time

1. **Answer the questions.**

a. Why should we eat food?

b. Name two foods that protect us from falling ill.

c. Name two foods that help build muscle strength.

d. Are you a non-vegetarian? What is your favourite food?

e. Why do we need water?

2. **Fill in the blanks with the correct words from the brackets.**

a. We must eat __________ kinds of foods. (same/different)

b. We get most of our food from __________ and animals. (soil/plants)

c. We must keep all the food that we eat __________. (uncovered/covered)

d. We should eat our meals at the__________ time. (right/any)

e. We must __________ our food properly. (swallow/chew)

3. **Indicate whether the following statements are true (T) or false (F).**

a. Potatoes, rice, bread and chapattis are known as body-building foods. ☐

b. We need only air and water to be healthy and strong. ☐

c. Fruits, vegetables and nuts protect us from illness. ☐

 ISBN 978-81-8477-926-4

d. We must only eat uncovered food. ☐

e. We must eat different kinds of food in the correct quantities. ☐

4. Give two examples of each.

a. energy-giving foods ____________ ____________

b. body-building foods ____________ ____________

c. protective foods ____________ ____________

5. Why should we eat breakfast?

Do you eat breakfast before going to school? Yes ☐ No ☐

We use energy even when we are asleep. We need to recharge our energy as soon as we wake up. This is why our body needs food in the morning even though we may not feel hungry.

Those who do not eat breakfast feel tired even in the morning. We all know that children who eat breakfast do better at school than those who do not.

What did you eat today? Make a list of what you ate and the food group to which it belongs.

meal	food	food group
breakfast		
lunch		
dinner		

 ISBN 978-81-8477-926-4

3
Living and Non-living Things

Our environment includes everything around us—land, air, water, forests, animals, plants and people. Some of these are living while others are not. All animals and plants are living things.

I Care...

Planting more trees ensures clean air for us to breathe.

Make three groups and go for a walk in the school playground.

group A	group B	group C
collect different types of leaves	collect different types of stones and pebbles	draw or write the names of insects and other small animals

All living things must have certain features in order to be classified as living beings.

 ISBN 978-81-8477-926-4

Characteristics of Living Things

Living things grow: All living beings take substances from their environment to obtain energy, to grow and to stay healthy.

growth

movement

Living things move: All living beings move. Some living beings show external movement as well—they can move from place to place by walking, flying or swimming. While other living beings show movement in response to light.

Living things breathe: All living beings exchange gases with their environment. Animals take in oxygen and breathe out carbon dioxide.

respiration

excretion

Living things remove waste: Excretion is the removal of waste from the body. All living beings need to remove waste from their bodies in the form of sweat, urine and poop.

Living things eat: When living beings feed, they gain energy; which is used in their growth. Animals eat plants or other animals, while plants make their own food using sunlight.

nutrition

 ISBN 978-81-8477-926-4

sensitivity

Living things react to changes: Living beings react to changes around them such as touch, light, heat, cold and sound.

reproduction

Living things reproduce: All living beings produce young ones. Humans make babies, cats produce kittens and pigeons lay eggs. Plants also reproduce. Many make seeds which can germinate and grow into new plants.

Non-living things do not display any of the characteristics of living beings. Sand, stone and glass are examples of non-living things.

Learn More

Look around your classroom and make a list of all the living and non-living things you may find.

Quiz Time

1. Answer the questions.

a. Give three examples of non-living things.

b. Give the differences between living and non-living things.

c. What is excretion?

d. Why do living beings need food?

e. Which gases do animals take in and breathe out?

 ISBN 978-81-8477-926-4

2. Tick (✓) the correct option.

		Yes	No
a.	Most living things move from one place to another by walking, flying or swimming.	☐	☐
b.	Living things feed and gain energy; which is used in growth.	☐	☐
c.	Non-living things reproduce or change into new substances on their own.	☐	☐

3. Write L for living things and NL for non-living things.

☐

☐

☐

☐

☐

☐

☐

☐

 ISBN 978-81-8477-926-4

4. Compare the chair and the cat. List their similarities and differences in the table below.

A chair is a non-living thing. It has four legs. This chair is brown in colour. It has a back. People use chairs to sit on. A chair cannot move on its own.

A cat is a living thing. It has four legs. This cat is white and grey. It has a back. People keep cats as pets.

similar	different

 ISBN 978-81-8477-926-4

4
PLANTS

Plants are the carpet of the Earth. There are so many plants on our planet that from outer space a large part of the Earth looks green.

Plants are useful to us in many ways. Humans and animals cannot survive without plants.

Plants are vital to our survival as they make oxygen that we need to breathe and food we need to eat. Some plants grow on land and some grow under water.

Observe the plants you see in your school and in your surroundings. Plants are of many sizes, shapes and colours. They can grow in very cold as well as very hot places.

Trees are big plants with strong stems called trunks such as gulmohar, banyan and mango.

banyan

apple

mango

 ISBN 978-81-8477-926-4

Factastic

Redwood trees are ancient giants, the tallest living beings on the Earth. They reach heights of up to 360 feet.

rose plant

Shrubs are small and bushy plants, for example, rose and hibiscus. They are also called **bushes**. Their height usually ranges from one to five metres.

Herbs have delicate stems and include plants such as mint, coriander and grass. They are mostly used to flavour or season food.

grass

coriander

What other herbs are used in your house?

____

____

dal garnished with coriander

 ISBN 978-81-8477-926-4

pumpkin

Creepers are usually found growing on the surface of the soil as they have weak stems. Examples of creepers are pumpkin and watermelon.

Climbers are plants with very weak stems. They wrap themselves around plants, rocks or man-made structures for support. For example, the money plant.

money plant

Factastic

Climbers move in either a clockwise or an anti-clockwise direction as they spiral around the support structure.

Plants are living things. They cannot move about like animals, but they grow. They need sunlight, air, water and soil to grow.

Explore

Keep a sunflower plant in the class. Place it where there is no direct sunlight. Keep changing the position of the plant every two–three days. Observe which way the flowers face. Draw or paste a picture of a sunflower.

 ISBN 978-81-8477-926-4

How a Seed Grows

Plants are living things. They cannot move about like animals, but they grow. They need sunlight, air, water and soil to grow. The length of time from the beginning of the development to the death of the plant is known as its **lifespan**. Each plant goes through its own stages of growth and development that may include seed, sapling and mature plant.

Parts of a plant include roots, stems, leaves, flowers and fruits. Leaves make food for the plant with the help of sunlight. Some parts of the plant grow under the soil and others grow above the soil.

sapling: a young plant or even a small tree, a seedling

 ISBN 978-81-8477-926-4

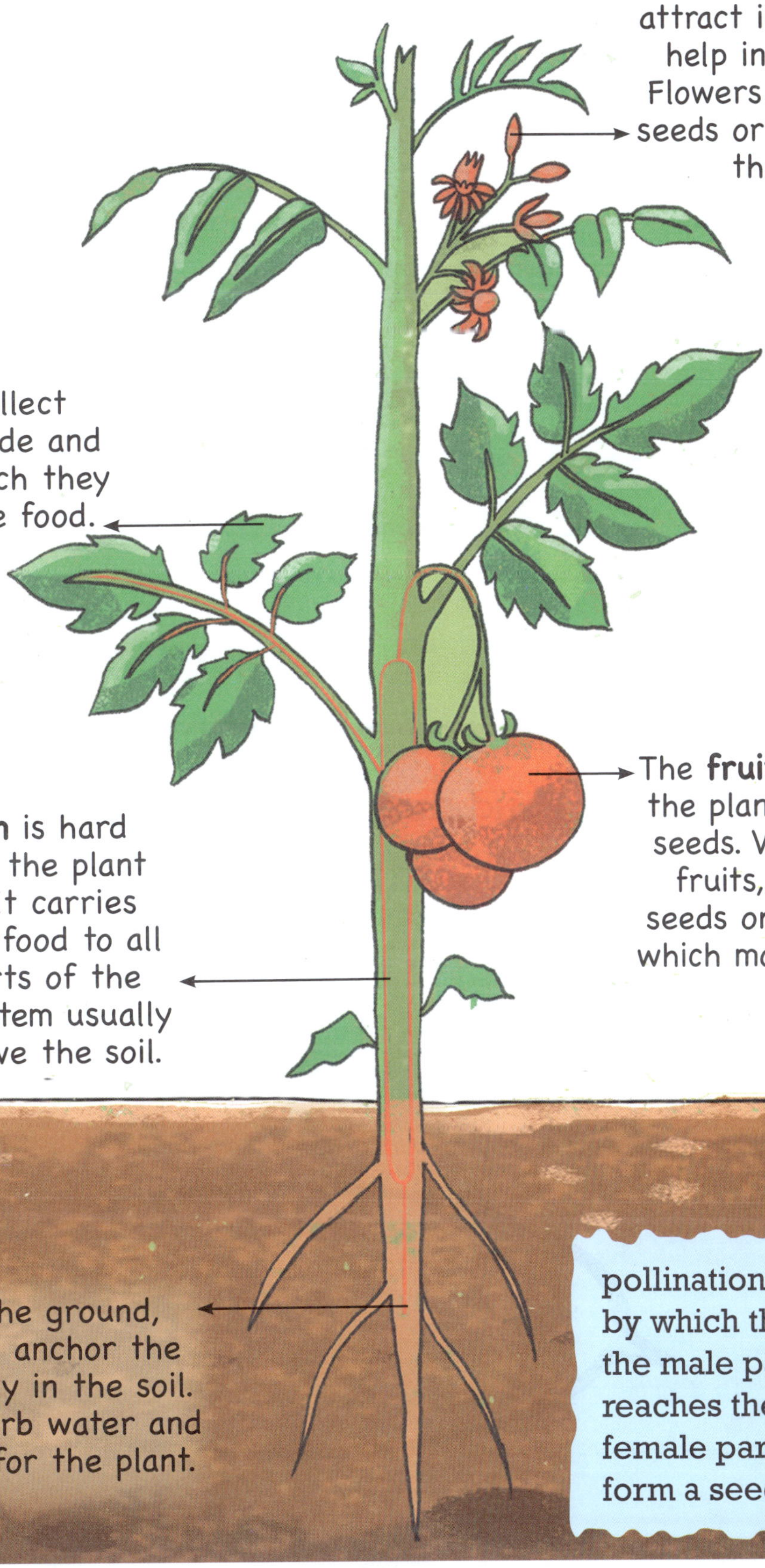

Flowers are colourful and scented to help attract insects, which help in pollination. Flowers produce the seeds or the fruits of the plant.

Leaves collect carbon dioxide and sunlight, which they use to make food.

The **fruit** is the part of the plant that contains seeds. When birds eat fruits, they scatter seeds on the soil, from which more plants grow.

The **stem** is hard and holds the plant upright. It carries water and food to all other parts of the plant. The stem usually grows above the soil.

Under the ground, the **roots** anchor the plant firmly in the soil. Roots absorb water and nutrients for the plant.

pollination: the process by which the pollen from the male part of a flower reaches the egg in the female part of a flower to form a seed

 ISBN 978-81-8477-926-4

Learn More

Place a cut celery stem in a jar of coloured water.

Colour the illustrations to show what you observe.

day 1	day 2	day 3

Circle Time

Observe the pictures and describe what is happening.
Discuss with the rest of the class.

Factastic

Some plants live for hundreds of years such as the banyan tree and the neem tree. Others, such as the cotton and the sunflower plant, live only for a few months.

 ISBN 978-81-8477-926-4

Explore

Look at the illustrations below and follow the instructions.

Separate one or two cloves from a bulb of garlic.

Pack the cloves carefully in the soil with the rounded end pointing downwards.

Place the pot in the Sun and water it every day.

Observe what happens.

day	observation
day 1	
day 2	
day 3	
day 4	
day 5	
day 6	
day 7	
day 8	
day 9	
day 10	

 ISBN 978-81-8477-926-4

Factastic

Plants grow from seeds. While some flowers grow into fruits, others do not. Fruits have seeds inside them. Some fruits have one seed, while others have more.

Plants as Food

Green plants make their own food by using sunlight, air and water. They make food only during the day. Plants store the extra food in their roots, stems, fruits, leaves and seeds. We eat various plant parts.

Seeds

Some seeds can be eaten. White beans, rajma, bengal grams and peas are examples of edible seeds.

white beans

wheat

rajma

rice

bengal grams

peas

 ISBN 978-81-8477-926-4

Stems

Stems usually grow above the ground, but some special stems, such as potatoes, grow under the ground. We eat stems such as sugar cane, potatoes, lotus stems and banana stems.

potato

sugar cane

Roots

Carrot, turnip and radish are roots.

carrot

turnip

radish

Leaves

Cabbage, spinach and lettuce are leaves that we eat.

cabbage

spinach

lettuce

 ISBN 978-81-8477-926-4

FLOWERS

The cauliflower, as its name suggests, is a group of flower buds, which can be eaten. Flowers of banana and drumsticks can also be eaten.

cauliflower

broccoli

FRUITS

We also eat pumpkin, tomato and lady's finger. These are actually fruits.

tomato

lady's finger

pumpkin

We also eat fruits such as oranges, pears and mangoes.

 ISBN 978-81-8477-926-4

Name the fruits.

Fruits can be crushed and squeezed to make beverages. Tea and coffee come from plants.

Plants give us spices such as chillies, coriander, fennel and cumin. Spices add flavour to our food and are obtained from the seeds, roots and bark of plants.

 ISBN 978-81-8477-926-4

Some Other Uses of Plants

cooking oil

paper

medicines

cotton and wool

bamboo

perfumes

rubber

jute

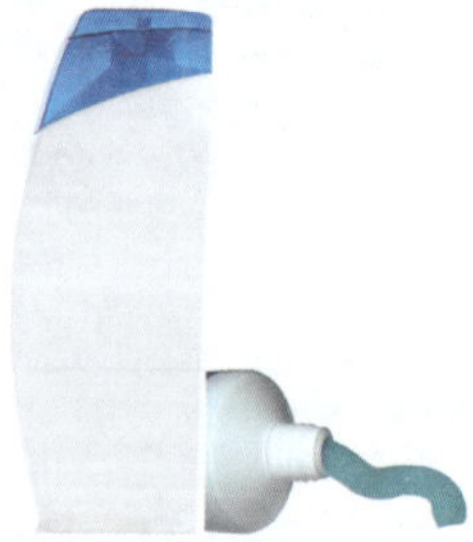

toiletries

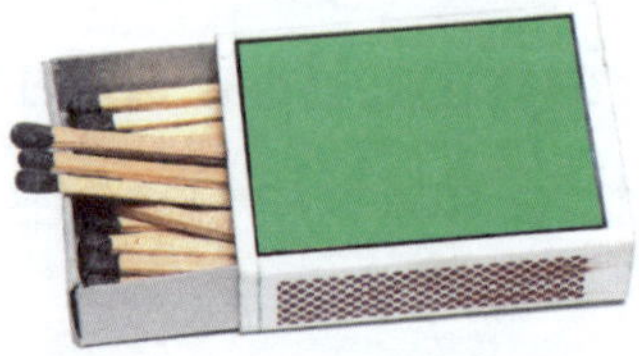

wood

 ISBN 978-81-8477-926-4

Plants keep our environment clean and green. Plants cause rain. We must not allow anyone to cut down trees, instead, we must grow more trees and plants.

Factastic

Bamboo can grow up to three feet in a 24-hour period.

Unusual Plants

Cacti grow in hot, dry places and require very little water to survive. They have thorns on their surface to stop animals from eating them. They also have thick stems to store water.

cacti

Mushrooms are not vegetables as they do not have any leaves, roots or seeds. They grow in damp places and do not need any light to grow. Mushrooms are a type of fungus.

mushroom

Carnivorous plants have special features that allow them to trap and digest insects. The venus flytrap and the pitcher plant are examples of carnivorous plants.

pitcher plant

venus flytrap

I Care...

Use paper sparingly. Use both sides of the paper.

 ISBN 978-81-8477-926-4

Quiz Time

1. Answer the questions.

a. What are bushes? Name two kinds of bushes.

b. What are climbers? Give an example of climbers.

c. Where do plants store their extra food?

d. Why do we need plants? Give five uses of plants.

e. How do cacti grow in hot, dry places?

f. How is a mushroom a unique plant?

g. What are the different parts of a plant that we can eat?

h. Give two examples of spices.

i. Why should we not allow anyone to cut trees?

2. Fill in the blanks with the help of words given below.

roots leaves stems seeds green

a. ______________ plants make their own food.

b. ______________ make food only during the day.

c. ______________ take the food to all the different parts of the plant.

d. Flowers of a plant produce ______________.

e. ______________ of a plant collect water and minerals from the soil.

 ISBN 978-81-8477-926-4

3. Find and circle the words from the box in the word grid.

wheat rice barley tea grapes pear beetroot turnip cauliflower spinach lettuce

a	b	t	j	b	j	f	w	a	w
c	e	l	k	a	u	s	r	w	e
a	e	e	g	r	a	p	e	s	r
u	t	t	h	l	i	k	u	y	f
l	r	t	b	e	k	l	i	u	s
i	o	u	f	y	j	t	o	l	z
f	o	c	s	w	h	e	a	t	c
l	t	e	a	g	g	a	p	k	f
o	e	t	u	r	n	i	p	k	d
w	r	y	e	h	p	e	a	r	t
e	t	s	p	i	n	a	c	h	s
r	r	i	c	e	f	o	l	p	q

4. Fill in the blanks with the correct words from the brackets.

a. ____________ is a group of flower buds. (Cauliflower/Radish/Cabbage)

 ISBN 978-81-8477-926-4

b. __________ is a leaf we eat.
(Spinach/Carrot/Potato)

c. Plants make their food during the __________.
(night/day/evening)

d. Some fruits have ________ inside them.
(seeds/roots/stems)

e. ________ hold the plant firmly in the soil.
(Stems/Roots/Fruits)

5. Name any four things that we get from plants, besides food.

6. Name two fruits that have one seed.

7. Name two fruits that have more than one seed.

8. Make a scrapbook of different types of leaves. Find out their names as well.

9. Label the plant parts in the picture.

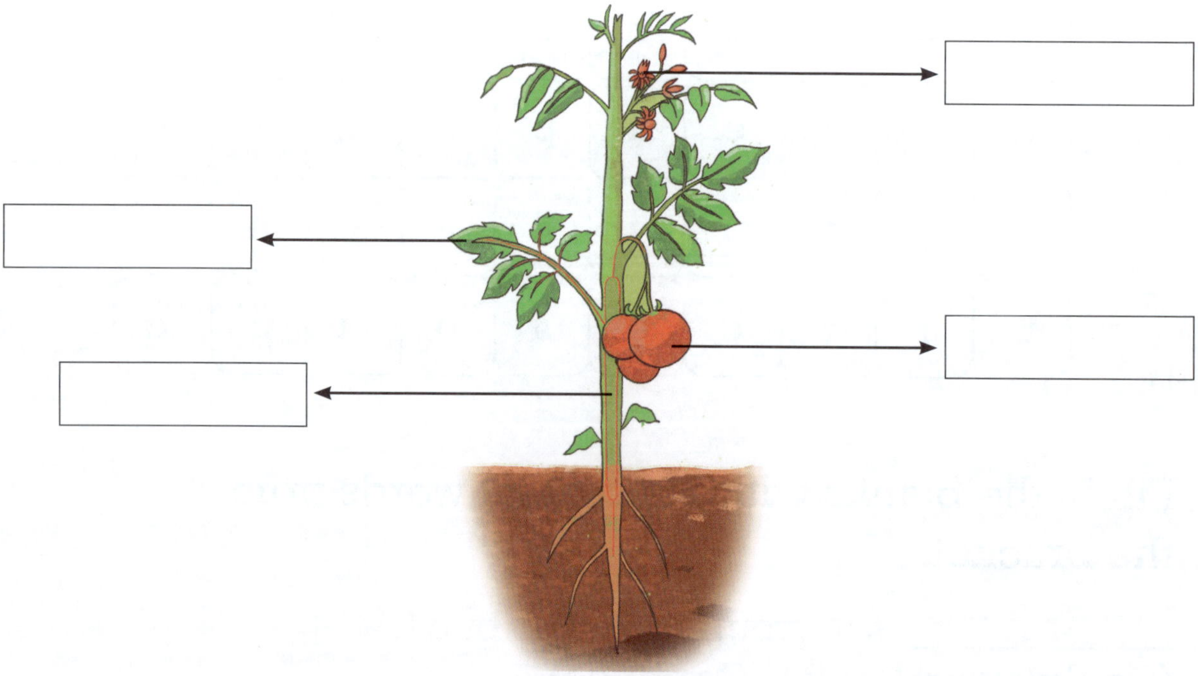

 ISBN 978-81-8477-926-4

5
Animals

Earth is the only known planet to have life on it. Animals are everywhere on Earth, from the highest mountain to the bottom of the deepest ocean.

cow

Polar bears live in very cold areas. Camels live in hot areas. Earthworms live under the ground. Bats live in caves and fly in the air. Sharks live in the oceans.

All animals need food to live. Animals can be classified into different categories based on their choice of food.

squirrel

Some animals eat grass and leaves. Others eat fruits and nuts. Such animals are called **herbivores**.

Factastic

Vultures and hyenas eat the remains of dead animals. They are known as scavengers.

lions

Some animals kill other animals and eat them. Such animals are called **carnivores**.

A **frugivore** is an animal that eats fruit. Frugivores have different ways of eating different fruit. Some use their teeth, while others use long or short beaks. Monkeys are an example of frugivores.

monkeys

Omnivores are animals that eat both plants and animals. For example, pigs, racoons and humans.

Explore

Go for a nature walk and observe the different types of birds you see. Write the names of three birds you see.

______________ ______________ ______________

Factastic

When animals die or are killed in large numbers, they become rare. They may then die out completely and become extinct. Some animals that are now extinct are dinosaurs and dodos.

 ISBN 978-81-8477-926-4

Circle Time

Find out the names of some animals that are rare to find in India. Discuss with the rest of the class.

ANIMALS AROUND US

Some animals can live on farms or in our backyards. They help us in many ways. These are known as **domestic animals**. For example, cats, dogs, sheep, goats, cows and horses. We can train some animals to work for us. Animals, such as donkeys, horses, elephants and camels, are known as **beasts of burden**.

We get wool from sheep, which is used for making woollen clothes.

Dogs help guard our homes. Dogs can also be trained to work as guides for the blind and to sniff out bombs and drugs as they have a very keen sense of smell.

We get milk from cows, buffaloes and even goats. Milk is used to make cheese, curd, ice cream and butter.

 ISBN 978-81-8477-926-4

The honey bee is very helpful to us. It takes nectar from flowers and makes it into honey.

Factastic

We get wax from beehives. This wax is used to make commodities such as candles and lipsticks.

We get eggs from ducks and hens. Eggs are high in protein.

Some of us eat fish, chicken and mutton. They are rich in protein.

Factastic

We get silk from cocoons of silkworms.

Explore

Visit a farm. Observe the animals there. What are the different animals used for?

Animals can get angry when protecting their young ones or territory. They may attack if they are hungry or because they are aggressive by nature.

 ISBN 978-81-8477-926-4

A wild boar may defend itself and its young by attacking. A rhino can easily trample anyone around that they consider dangerous.

Not just large animals, small animals can also be dangerous. Rats carry several infections that can be fatal to both humans and other animals alike.

I Care...

Do not buy products that have been tested on animals.

Learn More

Discuss how humans treat animals. Is it right to kill animals for food, for hunting or for testing in laboratories?

Quiz Time

1. Answer the questions.

a. What are beasts of burden?

b. What are herbivores? Give two examples.

c. How do dogs help us?

d. Name some animals that live on farms.

e. What are pet animals? Name three pet animals.

f. How are horses and camels useful to us?

g. How are cows and buffaloes useful to us?

 ISBN 978-81-8477-926-4

2. Classify the following animals as land animals, water animals and birds.

tiger whale goldfish parrot duck
pigeon octopus cow shark cat
crow bear giraffe lion

land animals	water animals	birds

3. Fill in the blanks with the help of words given below.

domestic frugivore eggs earthworms
donkey humans cow

a. The ________________ is a domestic animal.

b. We get ________________ from hens and ducks.

c. A ________________ carries heavy loads for us.

d. Dog is a ________________ animal.

e. A ________________ is an animal that eats fruits.

f. ________________ are omnivores.

g. ________________ live under the ground.

 ISBN 978-81-8477-926-4

4. Join the dots and match the young one to the adult.

6
Our Universe

The universe is a large expanse of dust, gas, stars, clouds, galaxies and other heavenly bodies.

The Sun, the Moon and the stars are all heavenly bodies.

The Sun

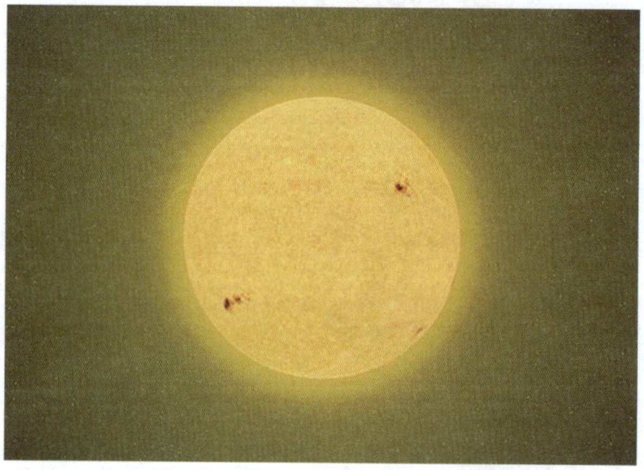

The Sun is a great ball of fire. It is the biggest and brightest body in our solar system. It looks small because it is very far away from the Earth. The Sun is about 150 million km away from the Earth. It gives us light and warmth. The Sun rises in the east and sets in the west.

I Care...

Do not look directly at the Sun as its brightness could damage your eyes.

The Moon

The Moon is the second brightest object that we see in the sky. Unlike the Sun, the Moon is not a star and hence has no light of its own. There is no air or water on the Moon. As a result, no life exists there. The Moon changes its shape every night.

 ISBN 978-81-8477-926-4

The pictures below show the different phases of the Moon.

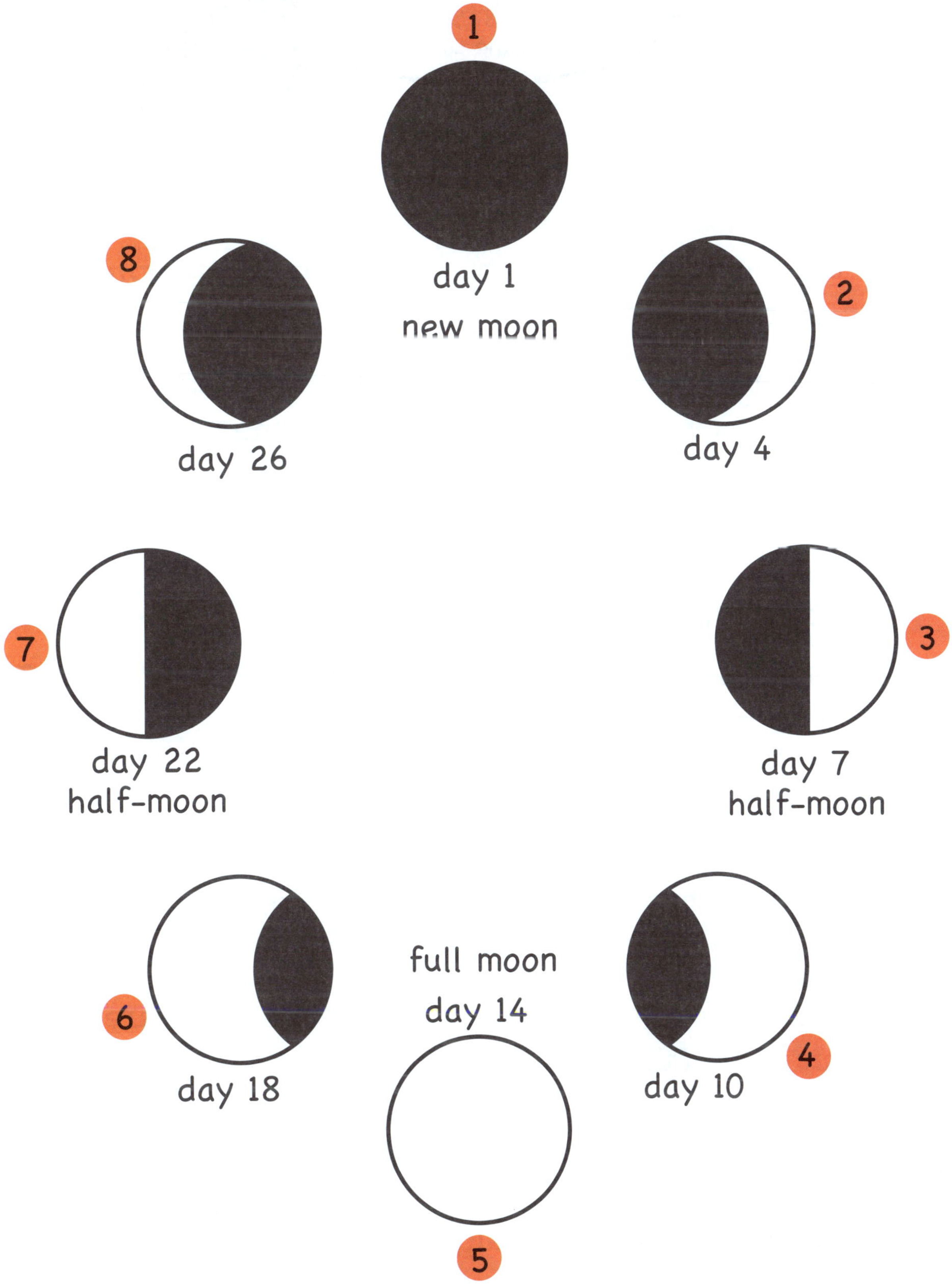

How many days does the whole cycle take? ______________

 ISBN 978-81-8477-926-4

Factastic

The Moon is 3,82,500 km away from the Earth.

Stars

A star is a giant mass of very hot, glowing gas. Stars produce their own light and energy.

There are so many stars in the sky that it is impossible for us to count them. New stars are being born all the time. Old stars also die. The Sun is the star nearest to the Earth.

Circle Time

Observe the night sky and share your experience with the rest of the class.

Day and Night

The day begins when the Sun rises in the morning. We wake up and get ready for school.

At midday or at noon, the clock strikes 12, while we are still at school. This is the middle of the day.

Most of us return from the playground as the Sun sets in the evening. We sleep at night, when it is dark outside.

At 12 o'clock at night, it is midnight.

 ISBN 978-81-8477-926-4

Day or night depend on the position of the Sun.
We do different things at different times of the day.
We use a watch or a clock to show us the time.

Look at the clock and write what you do at the times shown.

______________ ______________ ______________ ______________

Shadow

A shadow is formed when something comes in the way of light.

Take a thick book and place it in front of a torchlight or bulb.

What do you see? There will be a dark shape of a book on the wall. This dark shape is called a shadow.

 ISBN 978-81-8477-926-4

Explore

Stand outside in the Sun during different times of the day. Observe the size of your shadow for each time and record your observation in the table below.

time	size
morning	
noon	
afternoon	
evening	

A **calendar** tells us dates and days of all the twelve months of the year.

Name three months that begin with the letter J.

________________ ________________ ________________

Name the month that has three letters. ________________

Your birthday is in ________________.

Some months have thirty days while others have thirty-one. February is the shortest month with only twenty-eight days. There are fifty-two weeks and 365 days in a year.

There are 12 months in a year.

There are 52 weeks in a year.

There are about 4 weeks in every month.

There are 7 days in a week.

 ISBN 978-81-8477-926-4

There are 24 hours in a day.

There are 60 minutes in an hour.

There are 60 seconds in a minute.

It takes the Earth about 365 and a quarter days to go around the Sun once. We know that a year has 365 days. Every year the extra quarter day is carried over and in the fourth year we add it up to get one extra day in February known as the **leap day** (29 February). A year with an extra day in February is called a **leap year**.

Quiz Time

1. Answer the questions.

a. How many days are there in a year?

b. What do we get from the Sun?

c. Which star is nearest to the Earth?

d. How many months have thirty days? Name them.

e. How many months have thirty-one days? Name them.

2. Name the months.

a. The twelfth month of the year ____________________

b. The third month of the year ____________________

c. The fifth month of the year ____________________

d. The first month of the year ____________________

 ISBN 978-81-8477-926-4

3. Fill in the blanks with the help of words given below.

heat   Moon   dark   week   evening

a. The Sun gives us __________ and light.

b. There are seven days in a __________.

c. Nights are __________.

d. The __________ is seen at night.

e. The Sun rises in the morning and sets in the __________.

4. Indicate whether the following statements are true (T) or false (F).

a. The Moon is a great ball of fire, just like the Sun. ☐

b. The Sun is the star nearest to the Earth. ☐

c. It is impossible to count the number of stars in the sky. ☐

d. Life exists on the Moon. ☐

e. The Moon changes its shape every day. ☐

5. Fill in the blanks to complete the sentences.

a. There are __________ days in a week.

b. There are usually __________ weeks in a month.

c. __________ months make a year.

d. There are __________ weeks in a year.

e. The shortest month in the year, February has __________ days, except in a leap year when it has __________ days.

 ISBN 978-81-8477-926-4

6. Look at the Moon for a period of twenty-eight days and observe the shape of the Moon. Draw the various phases of the Moon.

7. Daytime starts as the Sun rises. It ends at sunset.

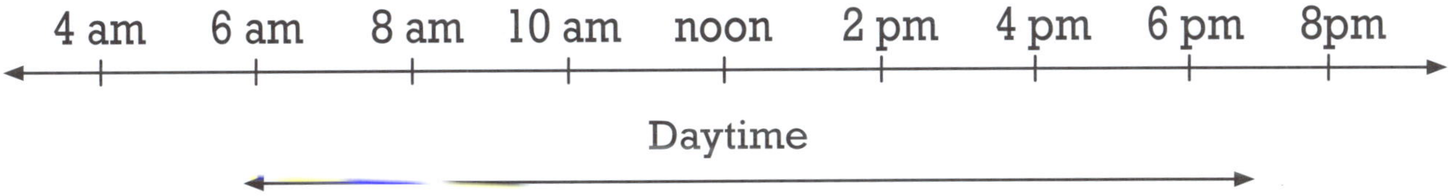

The Sun rises in the east at around 5.50 am.

The Sun sets in the west at around 6.30 pm.

The day begins as the Sun rises in the morning.

What time do you wake up to go to school? ____________

What time do you get back from school? ____________

What time do you go out to play? ____________

What time do you sleep at night? ____________

 ISBN 978-81-8477-926-4

7 EARTH

The Earth is shaped like a ball. It goes around the Sun and gets light and heat from it. The Earth is made up of land and water. Land covers one-fourth of the surface of the Earth. The remaining three-fourths are covered with water.

The blue region shows the oceans and the white areas are the continents.

Factastic

A globe is an accurate world map. Like the planet Earth, the globe is also shaped like a ball. All the countries are shown just the way they appear on the Earth.

 ISBN 978-81-8477-926-4

Circle Time

Find out information on Earth Day. Discuss with the rest of the class how you can participate to make a difference.

PHYSICAL FEATURES

Plains are flat lands. Many famous cities are in the plains. Crops grow well in the plains. Some parts are covered with forests. The plains are usually hot in summers and cold in winters. Many people live in the plains.

Deserts are large areas of land that are very dry and are usually covered with sand. There is very little water in a desert, and so very few trees grow there. Most commonly seen plants in deserts are cacti.

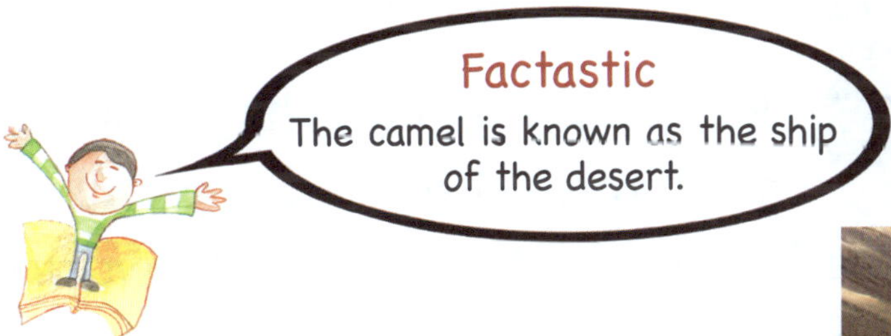

Hills and **mountains** are elevated rocky areas. They are much higher than the plains. Fewer people live in hilly regions than in the plains.

 ISBN 978-81-8477-926-4

High hills are known as mountains. It is very cold during winters in the mountains. High mountain peaks are usually covered by snow. As the snow starts to melt, rivers form in the mountains.

Explore

Have you ever visited any hill station? Write its name.

____

Valleys are the lowlands between mountains or hills. There are often thick forests in valleys. The land in a valley is fertile and good for growing crops. The climate is very pleasant. Valleys are usually densely populated.

A highland that is flat on top is known as a **plateau**. A plateau is also known as a tableland as its top looks like the top of a table. A plateau is usually rocky.

An **island** is land that is completely surrounded by water on all sides. The largest island in the world is Greenland. Some islands are their own countries such as Cuba, Iceland and Madagascar. The Andaman and Nicobar Islands and Lakshadweep Islands are a part of India.

I Care...

Keep your surroundings clean. If you see trash on the ground, throw it in a dustbin.

 ISBN 978-81-8477-926-4

Learn More

Find out the names of some of the islands around our country. Use a map or globe for assistance.

Quiz Time

1. Answer the questions.

a. What are valleys?

b. Describe a desert.

c. What is a highland with a flat top called?

d. What is an island? Name the largest island in the world.

2. Fill in the blanks to complete the sentences.

a. High hills are known as ____________.

b. Land covers ____________ of the Earth's surface.

c. We build ______ and canals to use surface water.

d. The ____________ is made up of land and water.

e. ____________ are the lowlands between mountains.

f. An ________ is a piece of land surrounded on all sides by water.

g. ________ are flat lands.

 ISBN 978-81-8477-926-4

8

Weather and Seasons

The Earth has a layer of air around it called the **atmosphere**. Changes in the atmosphere, such as the presence of clouds, winds and water vapour, make a place hot or cold. This is known as the **weather**. The weather changes every day. The weather can be hot or cold, cloudy or sunny, windy or rainy.

The **climate** of any place is the average weather of that place for many years. While the weather can change in a few hours, climate takes many, many years to change.

Learn More

Read the weather report in the daily newspaper.

  ISBN 978-81-8477-926-4

I Care...

We should dress appropriately according to the weather.

Explore

Maintain a weather record for five days. Tick (✓) the correct box to record the weather.

Monday	☐ 	☐ 	☐ 	☐ 
Tuesday	☐ 	☐ 	☐ 	☐ 
Wednesday	☐ 	☐ 	☐ 	☐ 
Thursday	☐ 	☐ 	☐ 	☐ 
Friday	☐ 	☐ 	☐ 	☐ 

 ISBN 978-81-8477-926-4

Season

The weather pattern changes a few times in a year. Such change in weather patterns is known as seasons. Seasons can be as short as two to three months or as long as six. Seasons can be hot, wet, cool or cold.

Summer, monsoon, autumn, winter and spring are the five important seasons in India. Some places, such as Pune in Maharashtra, experience the same weather throughout the year, with very slight changes. Other places do not really experience winter, for example, Chennai and Cochin in the south.

As India is a vast country, different parts of the country have different seasons at the same time of the year.

Summer

In India, the summer months are usually April, May and June. The Sun is hot and bright and the air is warm and dry. The days are longer than the nights. It is best to stay indoors and drink plenty of liquids during the hot summer days. We wear light cotton clothes to keep ourselves cool. We use fans, coolers and air conditioners to stay comfortable in summer.

Explore

What do you do in summer? How do you keep yourself cool and comfortable?

 ISBN 978-81-8477-926-4

Rainy Season

Cool winds from the sea bring rain clouds in July and August. The rainy season is known as monsoon. It is the wettest season of the year. Sometimes, we see a rainbow after it rains. Farmers pray for rains. Rains make the crops grow well. Rainwater fills up the rivers and lakes.

Autumn

Autumn is the period, generally September and October, just before the onset of winter. Trees shed their leaves in this season. It is neither too hot nor too cold in autumn.

Winter

In India, November, December and January are the winter months. The Sun shines, but not too brightly. Sometimes, there is fog and mist. It snows on the mountaintops. We enjoy hot food and drinks in winter.

Spring

Spring is a very short season in our country. Flowers bloom during spring. The air feels fresh. It is neither hot nor cold. Spring is also known as the queen of all seasons. February and March are the spring months. People go for picnics and outings during this period as the weather is very pleasant.

 ISBN 978-81-8477-926-4

Learn More

We do different things in different seasons. Match the pictures in Column A with the pictures in Column B.

Column A

Column B

 ISBN 978-81-8477-926-4

Learn More

Write what season it is in your city in each month.

Jan	Feb	Mar	Apr	May	Jun
Jul	**Aug**	**Sep**	**Oct**	**Nov**	**Dec**

Quiz Time

1. Answer the questions

a. What is atmosphere?

b. What are seasons?

c. Name the seasons that we experience in India.

d. What kind of clothes do you wear during summer?

e. Name the wettest season in India.

f. In which season do trees change colour and shed leaves?

g. Name the queen of all seasons.

2. Fill in the blanks to complete the sentences.

a. Changes in the ______________ are known as weather.

b. When a place has the same weather for a long period of time, it is known as the ___________ of that place.

c. There are ___________ seasons in a year.

d. The coldest season is ___________.

 ISBN 978-81-8477-926-4

9 AIR AND WATER

AIR

Air is all around us. We can feel it, even though we can't see it. All living beings need air to breathe.

Air contains small particles of dust. Observe the smoke that comes out of cars and buses. This smoke gets mixed with air. There are germs in the air that could make us ill. We must always cover our mouth when we cough, yawn or sneeze so that we do not spread germs.

When we dry clothes, the water in them evaporates into the air as water vapour.

Air is a mixture of gases, moisture and particles.

AIR POLLUTION

Since air is very important to us, we must try to keep it clean. With more cars on the roads, and more factories and industries, air pollution has increased a lot. Polluted air causes lung and skin diseases, and is harmful for birds, animals and trees as well.

 ISBN 978-81-8477-926-4

These are some things you can do to prevent air pollution.

- Plant trees to keep the air fresh and clean.
- If you are going to a place nearby, ride a bicycle.
- During Diwali, decorate your house with diyas instead of bursting harmful firecrackers.

Moving Air

We can feel the air when it moves. Moving air is known as **wind**. A gentle wind is known as a **breeze**. When the wind is strong and is blowing very fast, it is known as a **storm**. A strong wind can blow away things and can cause a lot of damage. A very strong wind is also known as a **gale**.

wind

breeze

storm

gale

Factastic

A wind gauge is used for recording the speed and direction of wind. It is also known as an anemometer.

 ISBN 978-81-8477-926-4

WATER

All living things need water. Look at the pictures and write how water is being used.

SOURCES OF WATER

Plants and animals need water to survive. We get water from rain, rivers, lakes and ponds. Rivers, lakes, ponds, wells, seas and oceans are different sources of water.

A small body of water is known as a **pond**. Ponds generally dry up during summers.

A large body of water is called a **lake**. It is surrounded by land on all sides.

The water we see on the surface of the Earth is known as **surface water**.

 ISBN 978-81-8477-926-4

We build dams and canals to use this surface water. Some of the rainwater is absorbed or seeps into the ground. This is known as **groundwater**. The water that we get in our taps comes from surface as well as groundwater.

A big channel of flowing water is known as a **river**. It starts from the mountains and then flows down to the plains. In the plains it moves slowly. There are many cities and towns along the banks of rivers. Rivers join the sea. **Seas** and **oceans** are very large bodies of water.

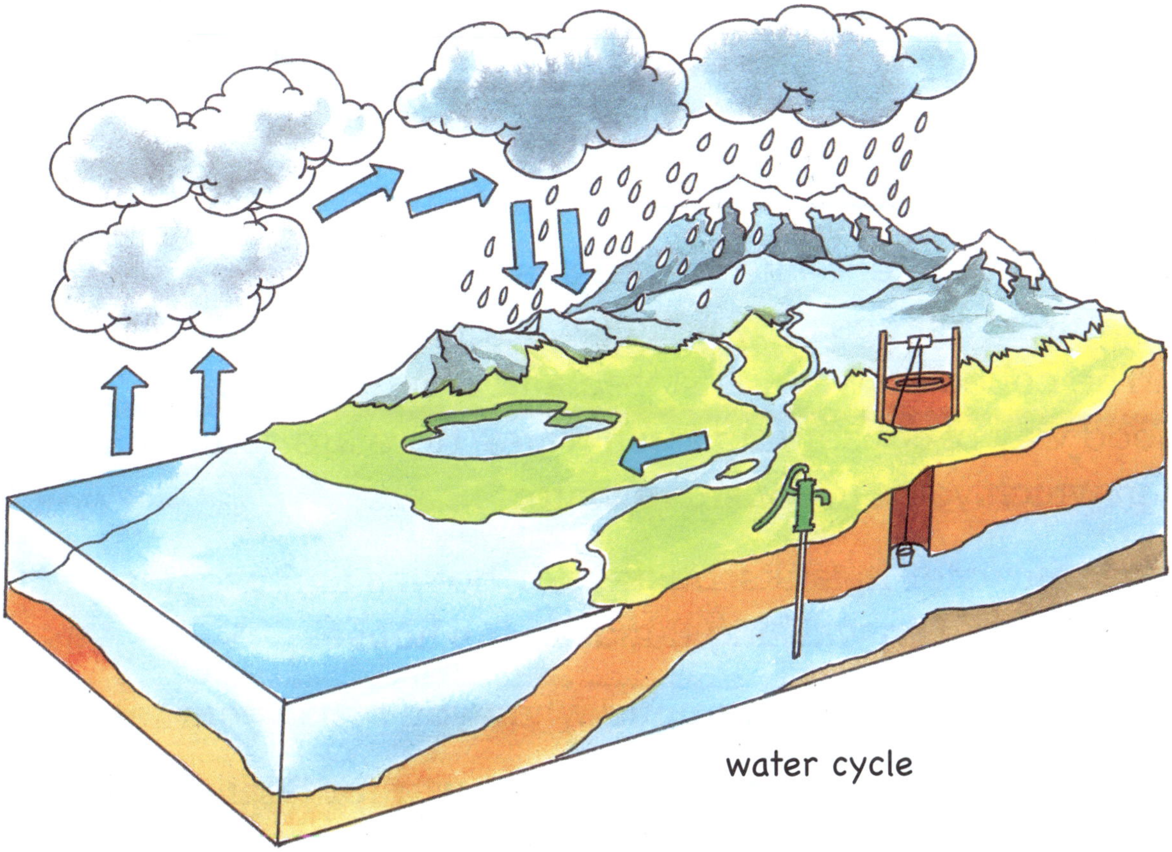

water cycle

All sources of water depend on rain. Therefore, rain is the main source of water.

When it rains, rainwater collects in the lakes, ponds and rivers. A large part of it also seeps through the soil and collects under the ground.

 ISBN 978-81-8477-926-4

Sea water is too salty to drink. We rely on fresh water (or non-salty water) from lakes, ponds, wells and rivers for domestic purposes. But we cannot drink this water directly as it is dirty and contains germs. Germs can make us sick. Water must be filtered and boiled for at least fifteen to twenty minutes to make it germ free.

Factastic

The water we use at home is usually rainwater and river water. The water is cleaned before it reaches our homes. We use different methods to purify water at home such as boiling and filtering.

Water Conservation

The Earth is our friend and we must take care of it. **Rainwater harvesting** is a process by which water is collected when it rains. The collected water is stored and can be used later. This is a good way of conserving fresh water. Here are some other ways in which you can conserve water.

- Store rainwater in tanks, buckets or bottles and use it later for cleaning and washing things in the house.
- Do not keep the water running when you brush your teeth.
- Use a bucket of water instead of a shower for taking a bath.

Explore

How can you help to save water in your daily life?

I Care...

Water is precious. It must not be wasted. Remember to close the tap after using it.

 ISBN 978-81-8477-926-4

Circle Time

Mohan stores water in tanks. He lives on a farm and needs a lot of water every day. What do you think he does with all the water?

Quiz Time

1. Answer the questions.

a. What does air contain?

b. Why do we need fresh air to breathe?

c. Name three sources of water.

d. Why do we need to conserve water?

e. What is air pollution? How can you help keep the air clean?

f. What are the ways in which we can conserve water?

2. Fill in the blanks to complete the sentences.

a. Moving air is known as ___________.

b. A _____________ is a big channel of flowing water.

c. A gentle wind is known as a ________.

d. ___________ water is too salty to drink.

e. A fast and strong wind is known as a _______.

f. ____________ air causes skin and lung diseases.

 ISBN 978-81-8477-926-4

3. Draw the water cycle. Label all the sources of water.

 ISBN 978-81-8477-926-4